OXYGEN CONCENTRATOR
BIOMEDICAL ENGINEERING

ATHEENA MILAGI PANDIAN

Copyright © Atheena Milagi Pandian
All Rights Reserved.

ISBN 978-1-63920-195-2

This book has been published with all efforts taken to make the material error-free after the consent of the author. However, the author and the publisher do not assume and hereby disclaim any liability to any party for any loss, damage, or disruption caused by errors or omissions, whether such errors or omissions result from negligence, accident, or any other cause.

While every effort has been made to avoid any mistake or omission, this publication is being sold on the condition and understanding that neither the author nor the publishers or printers would be liable in any manner to any person by reason of any mistake or omission in this publication or for any action taken or omitted to be taken or advice rendered or accepted on the basis of this work. For any defect in printing or binding the publishers will be liable only to replace the defective copy by another copy of this work then available.

ATHEENAPANDIAN PRIVATE LIMITED is basically a MEDICAL EQUIPMENT TRAINING platform to teach and share the Biomedical Engineering Science and Technology knowledge to all over the world through online and offline mode. Our incorporation is fully dedicated to the Biomedical beginners, freshers, academicians, corporates, researchers, and other Biomedical Engineering Passionates.

The Training Academy for Biomedical Engineers

We ask the indulgence of the biomedical youngsters and beginners who may read this book for dedicating it to a grown-up. We have a serious reason: they are the best engineers in the world. We have another reason: this grown-up understands everything, even books about biomedical engineering. We have a third reason: they live in a healthcare world where they are hungry for troubleshooting the medical equipment. They need cheering up. If all these reasons are not enough, we will dedicate the book to the biomedical engineers from whom this grown-up grew. All grown-ups were once biomedical engineers—although few of them remember it. And so I correct my dedication to Biomedical Beginners in the world.

Contents

Foreword — vii

Preface — ix

Acknowledgements — xi

Prologue — xiii

1. Introduction — 1
2. Oxygen Concentrator — 12
3. Principle Of Oxygen Concentrator — 15
4. Working Process — 16
5. How To Operate The Oxygen Concentrator — 21
6. Advantages Of Oxygen Concentrator — 23

Foreword

He is Atheena Milagi Pandian shortly Atheena Pandian from a traditional country India. He has been working hard to build his personal brand over the past 15 to 20 years. He was really interested in biomedical sciences especially in medical equipment calibrations, Biomedical updates, and Biomedical related fantasy literature. Medical equipment first appeared in his life when he was at the age of seven. Then he had got his first medical equipment as a Stethoscope. He always remembers himself thinking about it was the best thing in the world. He was often playing it whenever he could. but some time later, he really noticed that he could do a lot more things with his medical equipment, During his teenage, he has a passion for Biomedical Engineering and he plans to design some biomedical projects and research. Due to this impacts, he got under graduation and post-graduation degree in Biomedical Engineering from one of India's top university named as Anna university located in Chennai, then he felt to learn more in hospital management so he did his Master of Business administration in Hospital management and currently he is in the profession to create some quality biomedical engineer to the world.

By

Mr. A.S. ARUMUGA SAKTHI, Co-Founder, ATHEENAPANDIAN PRIVATE LIMITED

Preface

This is my pleasure to give this manuscript to all my Biomedical passionates, those who have a passion for the healthcare field, each and every day of life, every person has some disabilities while doing some work in-home or in the working sites, that unexpected disabilities maybe affect you physically, mentally and also it will disturb your personal life, but whatever it may be, the self-motivation is the best way to face everything, We are the biomedical engineers to help always to recover this uncomfortableness from peoples those who felt discomfort with their healthcare life.

This manuscript gives about the basic knowledge requirement of the healthcare field and its development. Our incorporation is always encouraging the people who have thoughts to recover the others illness by creating any medical devices. We will help the biomedical passionates by giving proper training on medical devices, which will encourage them to create some more helpful medical devices for society.

Basic knowledge about electrical and electronics, instrumentation, and human anatomy is the key to learn and understand medical devices.

Acknowledgements

My sincere thank to my God who gave me optimistic thoughts to do everything with confidence, I would like to express my special thanks of gratitude to my father Mr. P.A. Shanmuga Nathan as well as my mother Mrs. S.Saradhashanmuganathan who gave me the golden opportunity to do this wonderful profession and this profession make me do a good thing in my life which also helped me in doing a lot of manuscripts and I came to know about so many new things I am really thankful to them.

Secondly, I would like to thank all my family members, my wife Mrs. A. Sahaya Rooba, my son Master A.Aadhina Vignshwara Pandiyan, and my brother Mr. A.S.Arumuga Sakthi, helped me a lot in finalizing this idea within a limited time frame.

Thirdly, I would like to say my sincere thanks to Mr. Joel Samraj, Founder and Managing Director, AQUINIC, for his encouragement to do various activities.

Finally, I would like to say my sincere thanks to my co-authors Ms. Rashika Murugan and MsVennila Pandian, Biomedical Trainers, ATHEENAPANDIAN PRIVATE LIMITED (APPLD), for their content support and hard work.

Prologue

Push yourself, because no one else is going to do it for you.

Sometimes later becomes never. ...

Great things never come from comfort zones.

Dream it. ...

Success doesn't just find you. ...

The harder you work for something, the greater you'll feel when you achieve it.

Dream bigger.

CHAPTER ONE

Introduction

Oxygen

Atmosphere

- Oxygen is a non-metal element that is a gas at room temperature. Its molecules contain two oxygen atoms.
- Oxygen is vital for respiration, which is the process that transfers energy from glucose to cells.
- Oxygen is necessary for burning to occur. However, burning will only happen when the mixture of fuel and oxygen is hot enough.
- Oxygen is a non-metal element and is found naturally as a molecule. Each molecule is made up of two oxygen atoms that are strongly joined together.
- Oxygen has low melting and boiling points, so it is in a gas state at room temperature.
- When animals breathe in, oxygen molecules enter the lungs and pass through the lung walls into the blood. The blood carries oxygen to the cells of the body, where it takes part in a chemical reaction with glucose. This chemical reaction is called respiration.
- Respiration happens all the time in every living thing: it is how the cells receive energy. If an animal or plant does not have enough oxygen, it will not be able to respire and will die.
- If the temperature is high enough, many substances will burn in oxygen.
- When a substance burns, it reacts with oxygen: this happens in wood fires and also in car engines, which burn petrol.
- The chemical reaction transfers energy in order to make the engine work. The scientific word for burning is combustion.

Symbol of Oxygen

- It is found in the Earth's atmosphere, constituting 21% of the atmospheric volume.
- Oxygen along with its compounds accounts for nearly two-thirds of the mass of the human body and 49.2% of the mass of the Earth's crust.
- Oxygen (pronunciation: OK-si-jen) is a colorless element that belongs to the group of Chalcogens in the periodic table, and it is represented by the chemical symbol O.
- A highly reactive non-metal, it can easily form oxides with most of the other elements and their compounds.
- At room temperature, it is an odorless, tasteless diatomic gas characterized by the formula O_2.
- Oxygen gas is commercially extracted by fractional distillation of liquefied air.
- It can also be obtained by passing dry air through zeolite, a microporous mineral that can absorb nitrogen but leave oxygen.
- Passing the air through a selectively permeable ceramic membrane can produce highly pure oxygen.
- It can artificially be produced in the laboratory by using manganese (IV) oxide as a catalyst to decompose aqueous hydrogen peroxide or by electrolytic decomposition of water.
- Oxygen is also formed when potassium chlorate ($KClO_3$) is heated strongly.

Oxygen in Human Lungs

The amount of oxygen consumed by the lung itself is difficult to measure because it is included in whole-body gas exchange. It may be increased markedly under pathological conditions such as lung infection or adult respiratory distress syndrome. To estimate normal oxygen consumption of the human lung as a basis for further studies, respiratory gas analysis during total cardiopulmonary bypass may be a simple approach because the pulmonary circulation is separated from systemic blood flow during this period.

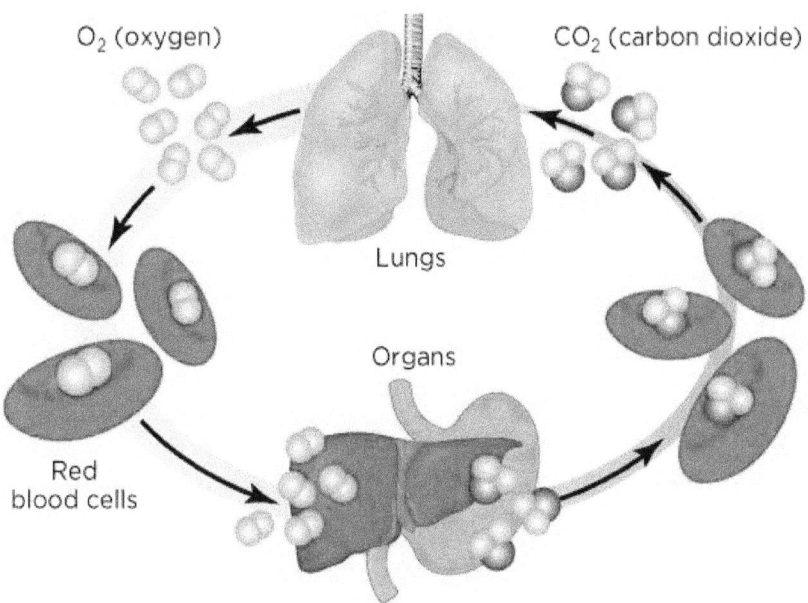

Oxygen in the Lungs

The human lung consumes about 5-6 ml oxygen per minute at an esophageal temperature of 28 degrees C. Prebypass whole-body oxygen consumption measured at nearly normothermic conditions was 198 +/- 28 ml/min. Mean lung and whole-body respiratory quotients were similar (0.84 and 0.77, respectively). Extrapolating lung oxygen consumption to 36 degrees C suggests that the lung consumes about 11 ml/min or about 5% of total body oxygen consumption. Because the amount of enflurane diffused from the systemic circulation into the bronchial system during cardiopulmonary bypass was less than 0.1%, the contribution of bronchial blood flow to lung gas exchange can be assumed to be negligible.

Our respiratory system comprises a conduction zone and a respiratory zone. The conduction zone brings air from the external environment to the lungs via a series of tubes through which the air travels. These are the:

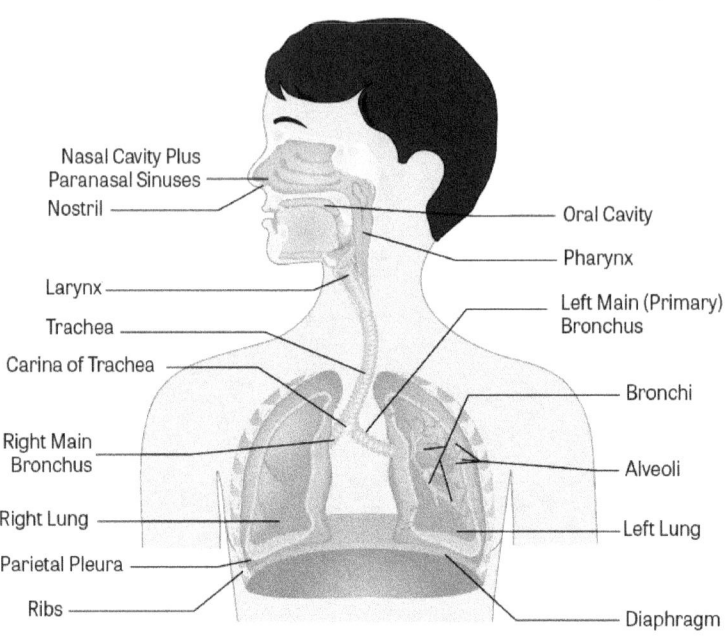

Parts of Respiratory Tract

1. Naal cavity;
2. Pharynx (part of the throat behind the mouth and nasal cavity),
3. Larynx (voice box),
4. Trachea (windpipe);
5. Bronchi and bronchioles.

Aside from conducting air to the lungs, these tubes also:

1. Warm the incoming air;
2. Filter out small particles from it;
3. Moisten it to ease the gas exchange in the lungs.

The nasal cavity has a large number of tiny capillaries that bring warm blood to the cold nose. The warmth from the blood diffuses into the cold air entering the nose and warms it.

The lining of the pharynx and larynx (which form the upper respiratory tract) and the lining of the trachea (lower respiratory tract) have small cells with little hairs or cilia. These hairs trap small airborne particles, such as dust, and prevent them from reaching the lungs.

The lining of the nasal cavity, upper respiratory tract and lower respiratory tract contains goblet cells that secrete mucus. The mucus moistens the air as it comes in, making it more suitable for the body's internal environment. It also traps particles, which the cilia then sweep upwards and away from the lungs so they are swallowed into the stomach for digestion, rather than getting trapped in the lungs. This mechanism of moving trapped particles in this way is known as the mucociliary escalator.

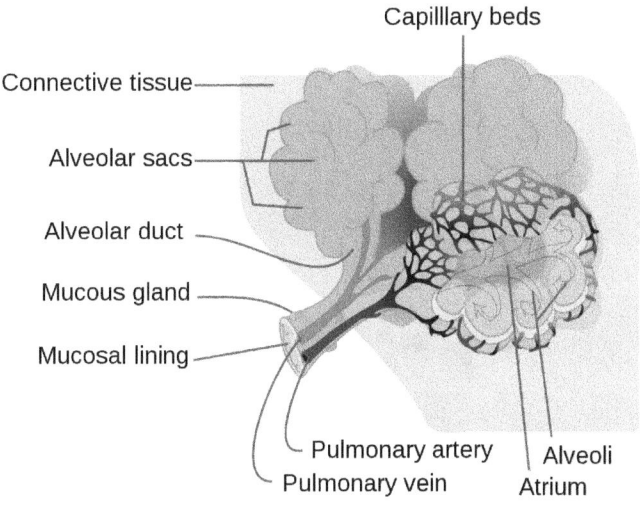

Alveoli

The lungs are a little like balloons: they do not inflate by themselves, but only do so if air is blown into them. We can blow into the lungs and inflate them – which is one of the two techniques used for cardiopulmonary resuscitation – but that does not happen in the normal daily life of healthy people. We have to inhale and exhale air by ourselves.

Problems without Oxygen

Asthma

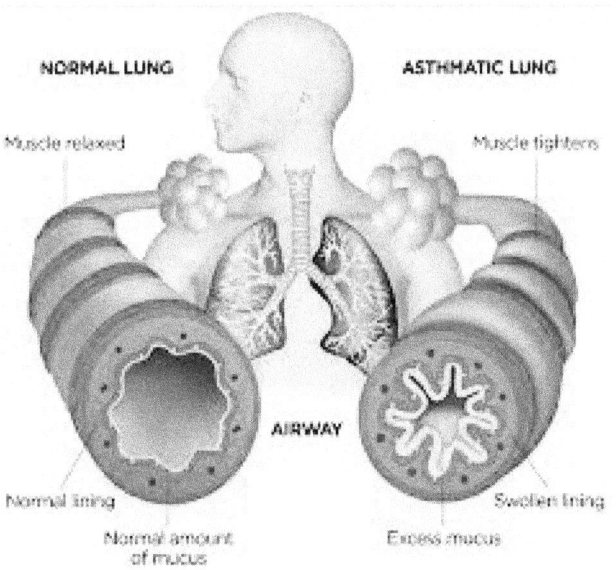

Affected Lungs

Asthma is one of the diseases that affect the airways. It is called a long-term disease of the lungs and is termed a chronic respiratory disease. Asthma causes breathing problems because your airways become narrow due to inflammation. For some people with chronic asthma, it can be difficult to talk or lead an active life.

Chronic Obstructive Pulmonary Disease

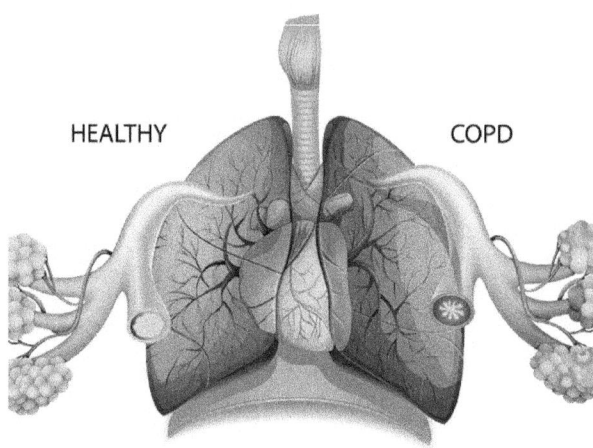

Chronic Obstructive Pulmonary Disease

Chronic Obstructive Pulmonary Disease is commonly known as COPD. It is another long-term lung disease that is one of the main breathing problems causes. People who have either one or more types of the following conditions are said to have COPD. The conditions are chronic bronchitis, emphysema, or refractory asthma.

Emphysema

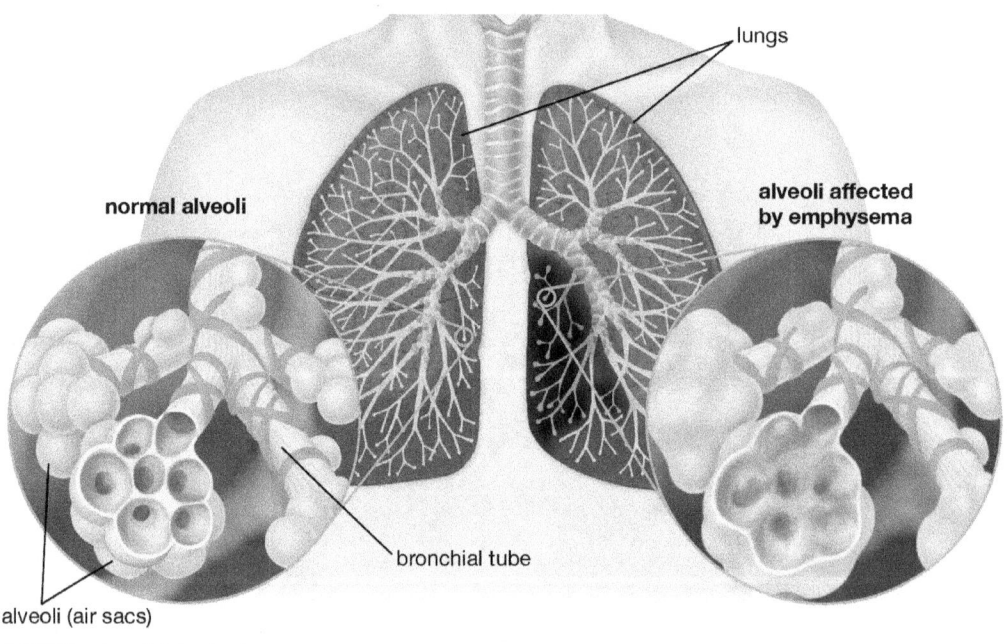

Emphysema

A type of COPD, emphysema is a chronic respiratory disease. Here, air pockets are formed in the lungs whereby air is blocked inside these pockets. This is caused due to destruction of tissues that are found in the air sacs. This causes the lungs to become bigger and it leads to difficulty in breathing; another term used for emphysema is airflow limitation.

Chronic Bronchitis

Chronic bronchitis is when the air tubes in the lungs get inflamed and irritated. In chronic bronchitis, you can be coughing for at least three months or even up to 2 years. Chronic bronchitis is another long-term respiratory illness that can be recurring and doesn't just go away. It is one of the types of COPD.

Cystic Fibrosis

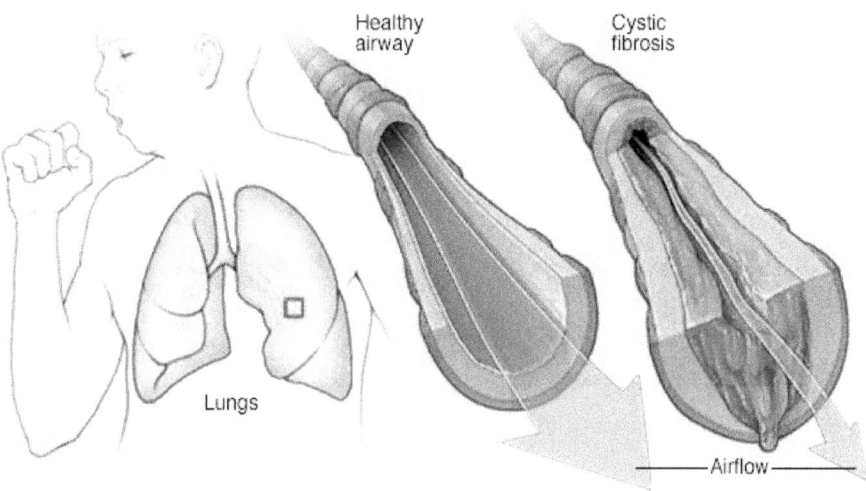

Cystic Fibrosis

Cystic Fibrosis is a genetic condition. When mucus forms in the bronchi, it should be cleared so that there are no Breathing Problems. However, when this does not happen, it can lead to a build-up of mucus in the bronchi which causes cystic fibrosis. In this condition, you will be prone to lung infections, repeatedly.

Pneumonia

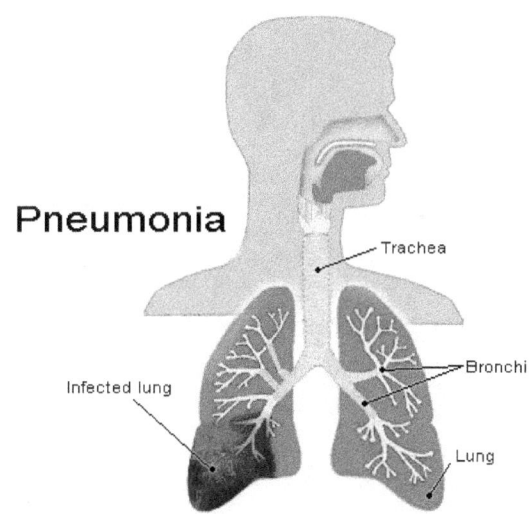

Pneumonia

Pneumonia is caused when the air sacs in the lungs are filled with either pus or fluid. This causes breathing difficulties because insufficient oxygen is present in your blood. It is called a lung infection, which can be severe or mild. Young children who are less than two, and the elderly, are most likely to have this infection.

Tuberculosis

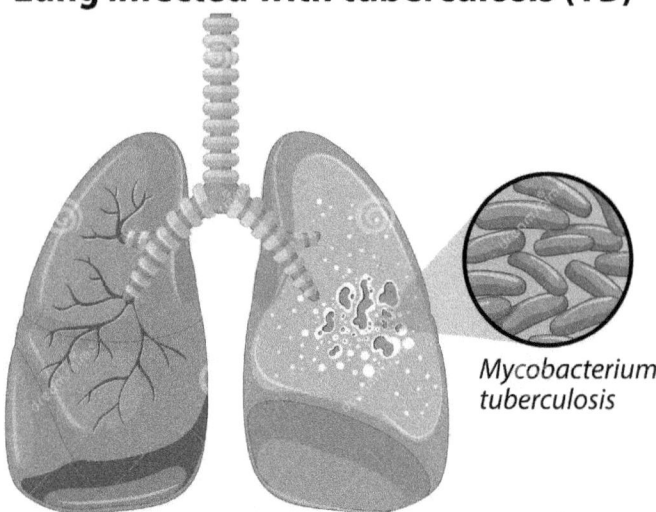

Tuberculosis

Tuberculosis was also known as TB, and it affects your lungs. Tuberculosis is caused by bacteria known as Mycobacterium Tuberculosis. It is a contagious disease and it can easily spread to various parts of the body, such as the spine. There are two forms of TB called active TB and latent TB.

Pulmonary edema

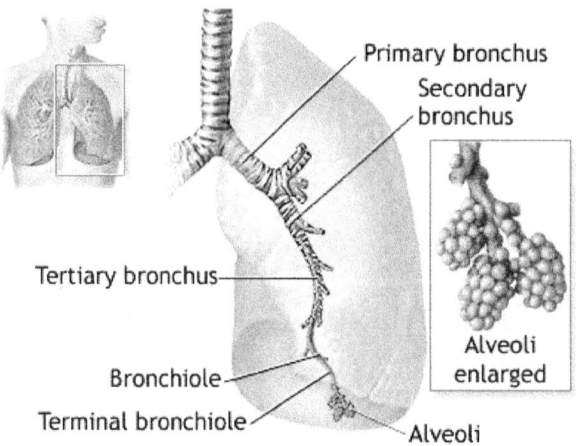

Pulmonary edema

Pulmonary edema occurs due to fluid leakage. Many small blood vessels can be found in the lung. When the fluid leaks from these vessels and goes into the air sacs and areas that are close-by, then it is called pulmonary edema. This can be caused due to lung injury or due to heart failure.

Lung Cancer

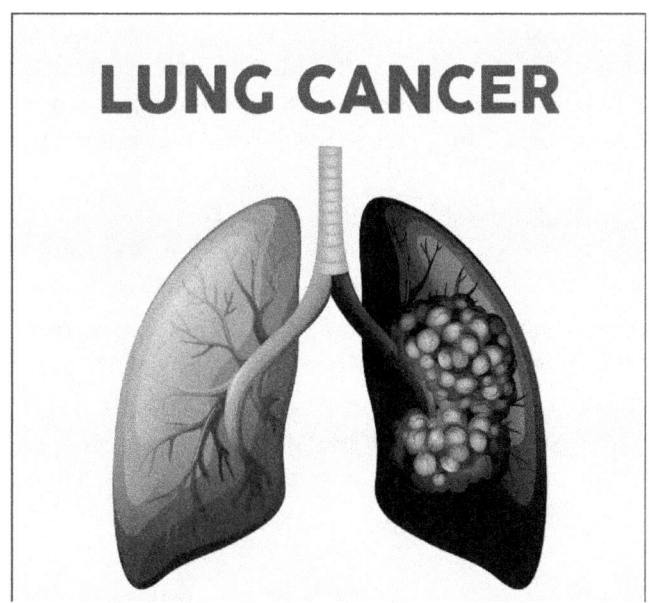

Lung Cancer

Lung cancer can develop in any area of your lungs. Normal lung cells perform many functions and help build lung tissues. In lung cancer, abnormal cells grow rapidly in one or both of your lungs. These abnormal cells do not perform any functions of normal lung cells. It usually develops near the air sac area or inside the air sacs.

Interstitial Lung Disease

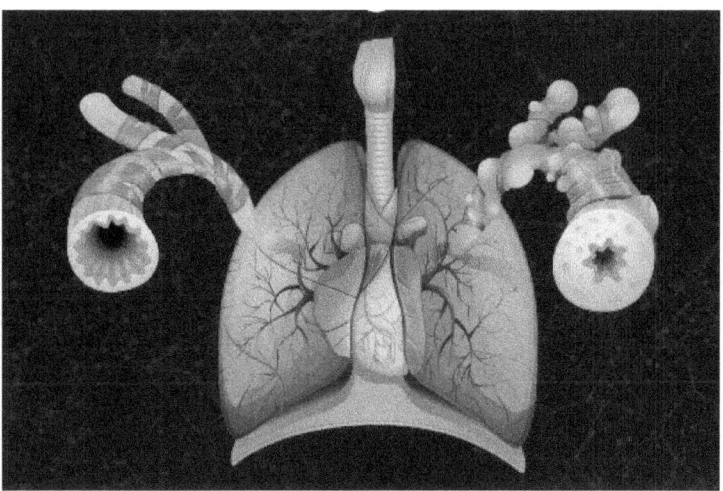

Interstitial Lung Disease

Interstitial lung disease is commonly known as ILD. It is an umbrella term used to describe several types of lung conditions. ILD affects the interstitium by causing it to thicken. This can be due to a buildup of fluid, inflammation, or scarring. ILD can be short-term or long-term. There are various types of ILD including hypersensitivity pneumonitis and cryptogenic organizing pneumonia.

Risk Factors of Lack of Oxygen

The following are some of the risk factors for respiratory disease.

1. Long-term cigarette smoking is one of the biggest risk factors for lung-related problems and respiratory disease.
2. Household chemical cleaners can be one of the risk factors of respiratory disease.
3. Some types of respiratory equipment can increase the risk of respiratory problems as there is a chance of breathing in dust along with air.
4. Houseplants can increase the risk of respiratory disease
5. When there is poor air circulation, then there is a higher chance that you will have a respiratory problem.
6. Mould and mildew in the bathroom can increase the risk of respiratory system problems.
7. Aerosol products can further aggravate mild symptoms in people and can increase the risk of lung problems.
8. Asbestos and radon gas are risk factors and can lead to respiratory problems.
9. Wherever there is an accumulation of fumes, it can increase the chances of respiration-related health problems.
10. Fireplaces can increase the risk of developing respiratory problems.
11. Dust and dirt accumulation can cause many people to have respiratory-related problems and can lead to lung problems too.

Diagnosis of Respiratory disorders

Respiratory diseases can be diagnosed using one or more of the following methods.

- Lung function tests are known as pulmonary function tests too. These help to determine whether your lungs are working optimally or not. They help to see how well air movement is taking place, how much air the lungs can hold, and how efficiently the lungs can move the oxygen into the bloodstream. There are various types of lung function tests such as lung volume test, exercise stress test, spirometry, and gas diffusion test.
- A chest x-ray is a type of imaging test. It makes use of electromagnetic waves to create images of the area inside and outside your chest. Chest x-rays are used to diagnose lung and respiratory conditions such as lung cancer, fibrosis, pneumonia, and tuberculosis. They can be used for monitoring conditions and can be used after surgeries too.
- Chest MRI is also known as the Nuclear Magnetic Resonance test. This is an imaging test that makes use of a computer, radio waves, and magnets to create images that show details of your chest. It shows a detailed view of your heart, blood vessels, and chest wall. Chest MRI can be done after CT scans and chest X-rays. It helps to diagnose various types of lung problems such as blood vessel problems and pleural disorders.
- Lactate Dehydrogenase (LDH) Isoenzymes Test is a test used to measure the level of isoenzymes that are present in your blood. The LDH test is used to determine information about tissue damage. It helps to find the type of tissue damage that has occurred, the location of the tissue damage, and the severity of the tissue damage.
- Bronchoscopy is one of the tests that are used to determine the cause of the lung problem. It helps take a look into the lung's airways by inserting a bronchoscope tube through your mouth or nose. Bronchoscopy can help diagnose mucus in the airways, blockages, and bleeding in the lungs. It can determine signs of infection and can help detect tumors as well. A chest x-ray might be done after bronchoscopy.
- Needle biopsy of the lung is required when imaging tests are unable to reach certain nodules in the lung. Needle biopsy is a test that takes a tissue sample from the lung that can then be examined under a microscope. It is considered a less invasive procedure than a surgical biopsy and it helps determine whether a nodule is cancerous or non-cancerous.

Basic Respiratory Medical Devices

- Air Cleaners.
- CPAP Machines.
- BiPAP Machines.
- Portable Emergency Oxygen Systems.
- Nebulizers.
- Pulse Oximetry Meters.
- Home Oxygen Concentrators.
- Portable Oxygen Cylinders.
- Suction pumps and more

Here in this manuscripts, we are going to detail about the oxygen concentrator is a Non-invasive therapeutic medical device that is used to deliver oxygen to individuals who are suffering from respiratory ailments like COPD (Chronic Obstructive Pulmonary Disease), Asthma, Pneumonia, COVID-19, late-stage heart failure, cystic fibrosis, Sleep Apnea. Our body can't survive the absence of oxygen which can affect breathing (shortness of breath), lung diseases, and some medical complications. The absence of oxygen also affects the functions of the heart, brain, and other organs in our body. This device is used as an oxygen supplement to the above-mentioned respiratory ailments. The oxygen concentrator is also called oxygen gas generators or oxygen generation plants.

CHAPTER TWO

Oxygen Concentrator

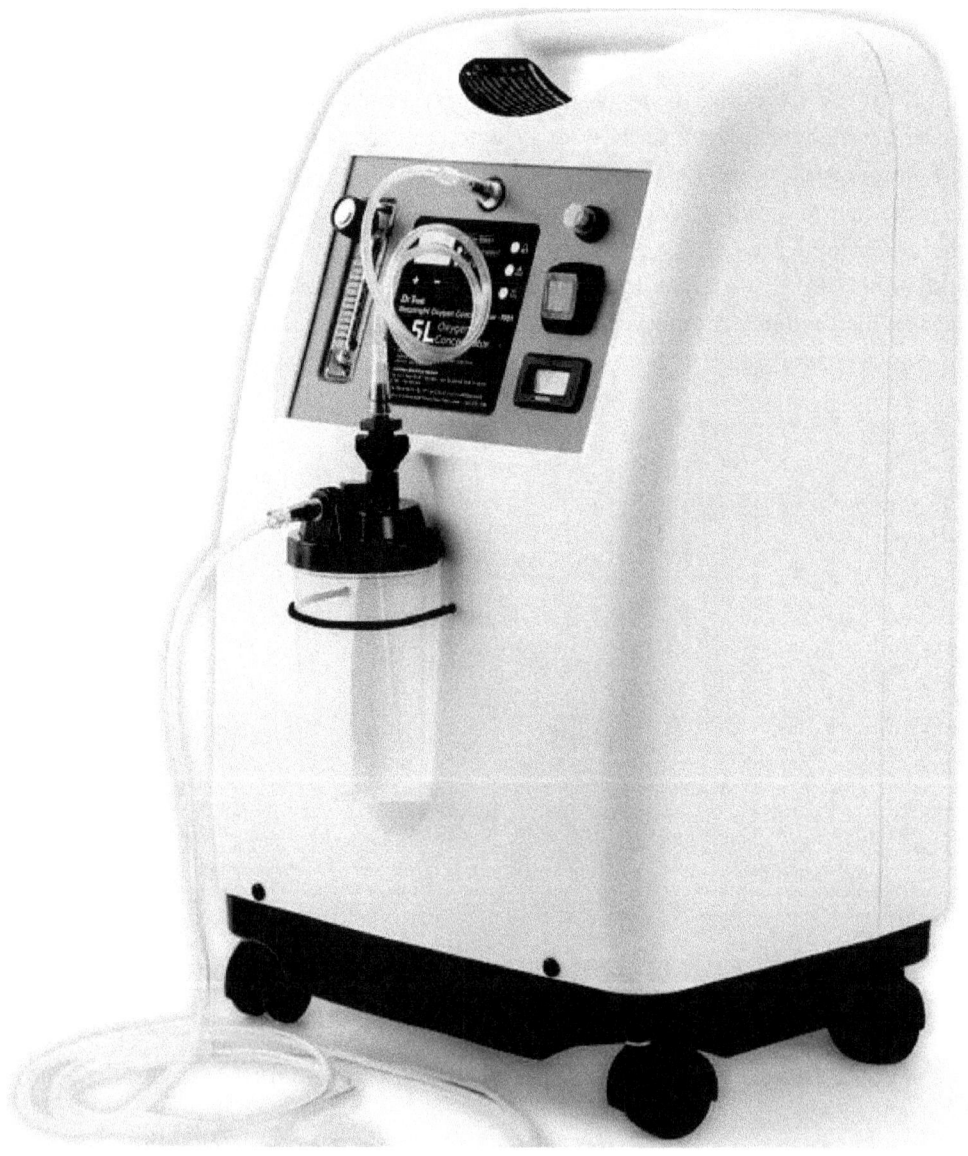

Oxygen Concentrator

- Primarily after 1772 Carl Wilhelm Scheele who is a Swedish chemist was discovered oxygen molecule. Joseph priestly an English chemist who was discovered oxygen molecule in 1774 but he published his research three years before Carl Wilhelm Scheele.

- After century scientists and doctors to discover the purpose of oxygen in the medical field and how important oxygen to treat varying illnesses and diseases. In 1885, the first usage of oxygen was recognized for a medical purpose. This medical purpose was to treat pneumonia patients.
- In the twentieth century, the connection of oxygen to the patient could be done by a nasal catheter which is a tube-like structure inserted into the nose for delivering the oxygen. During the first world war, the gas mask was invented by John Scott Haldane in 1917, to protect and treat soldiers who had been affected by dangerous chlorine gases.
- The first form of oxygen therapy is used strictly in ambulances and medical emergencies was invented in the 1950s. The revolution of oxygen therapy has been developed in the 1970s. Portable oxygen concentrators have been broadly available since the 1970s and the use of portable oxygen concentrators in homes also available but the usage of oxygen concentrators had been a limited period and also highly expensive.
- The advancement of oxygen therapy contains an oxygen tank that is extremely large and heavy compared to now. That oxygen tank carries purified oxygen within itself. In the next 30 years, the size of oxygen concentrators began to reduce because of the demand by youngers who have been affected by respiratory diseases.
- At present oxygen concentrators are small and fit in a purse, under the seat on an airplane, and also can able to bring bike riding. Nowadays some concentrators have a weight of fewer than 3 pounds and 10 hours of battery life and have an output of oxygen level is 10 liters per minute.

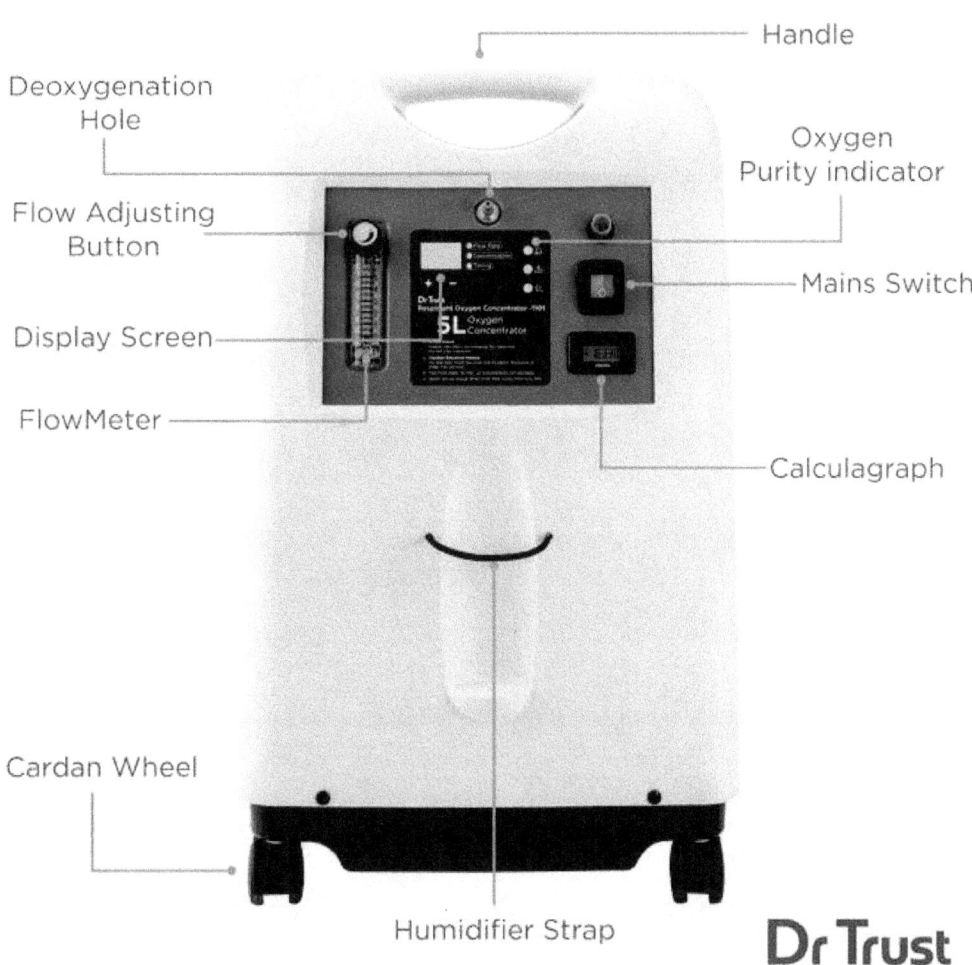

Parts of Oxygen Concentrator

CHAPTER THREE

Principle of Oxygen Concentrator

PRINCIPLE OF OXYGEN CONCENTRATOR:

The principle of O_2 concentrator is
1. Pressure swing adsorption
2. Membrane gas separation

Pressure swing adsorption:

The principle of pressure swing adsorption is a process used to separate some gas types from a mixture of gases under high pressure, due to high pressure the more gases absorbed. PSA method involves the process of absorption of the oxygen gas from the atmospheric gas with the help of adsorbent material such as Zeolite.

ZEOLITES:

Zeolite is a micropore crystallite Aluminosilicate mineral that contains aluminum and silicon component, which act as a drying agent in air and water purification. The two main properties of Zeolite is
1. adsorption
2. ion exchange.

The property of adsorption is used in air purification. Adsorption is a process in which the substances used for adsorption is called adsorbent.

Membrane Gas Separation:

Membrane gas separation is the principle that is responsible for the separation of gas mixtures by a synthetic membrane. The synthetic membrane is made up of polymers and ceramic materials. In polymers such as polyamide or cellulose acetate are used to produce synthetic membrane. The membrane act as a permeable barrier which different compounds move across at different rates or do not cross at all. The performance of the membrane is based on permeability and selectivity. In membrane gas separation method usually pumps gas into the membrane and the needed gas is separated depends on the difference in diffusivity and solubility.

In an oxygen concentrator, the membrane gas separation method occurs inside the zeolite which absorbs nitrogen from the compressed air and releases 96% pure oxygen to the oxygen tank.

Descriptions

Oxygen concentrators are medical devices that assist people who have a low level of oxygen in their blood. They are powered by plugging the device into an electrical outlet or by using a battery. If a battery is used, then it will need to be charged by plugging it into an electrical outlet. Most concentrators also come with an adapter so you can use the device while you drive.

An oxygen concentrator receives air, purifies it, and then distributes the newly formed air. Before it goes into the concentrator, air is made up of 80 percent nitrogen and 20 percent oxygen. An oxygen concentrator uses that air then it comes out as 90 to 95 percent pure oxygen and 5 to 10 percent nitrogen. The nitrogen is separated to give the patient the highest dose of oxygen possible, as it is difficult to get that percentage of oxygen without the help of a medical device.

CHAPTER FOUR

Working Process

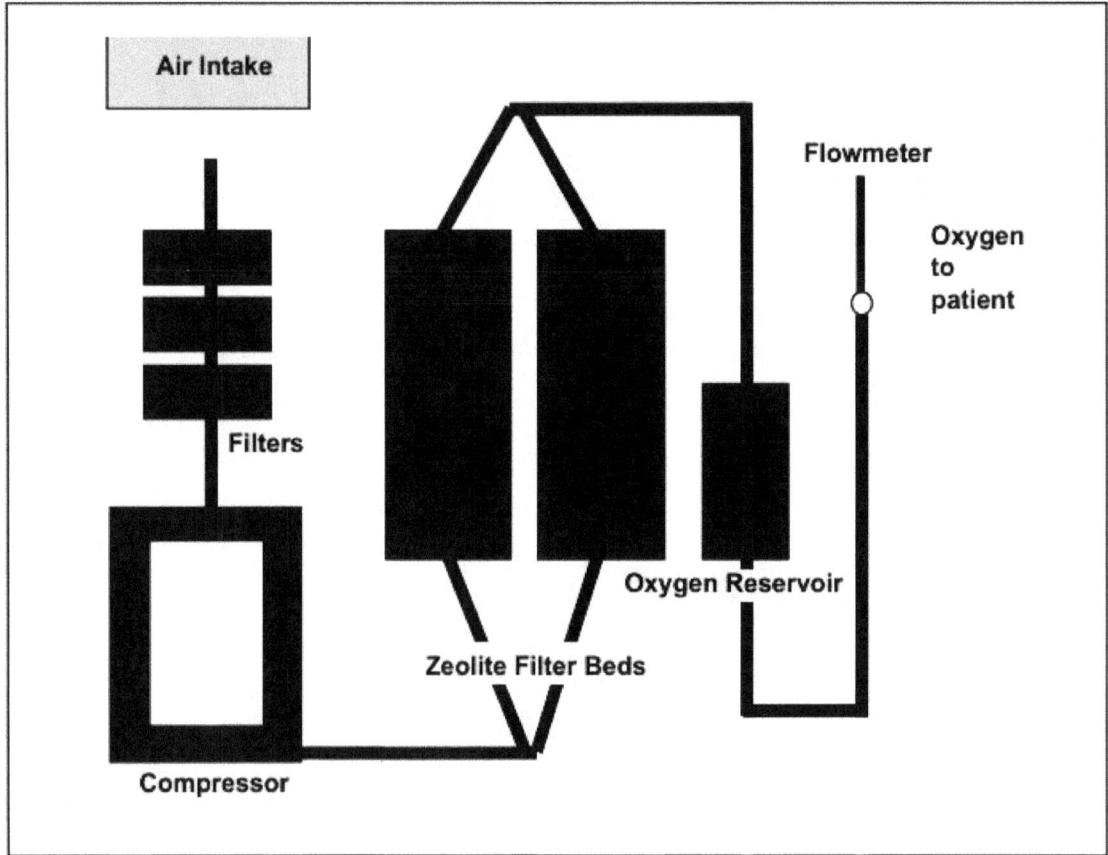

Schematic view of Oxygen Concentrator - (thanks iambiod website)

The 5 Step Concentrator Process:
1. Takes air from the room.
2. Compresses the oxygen.
3. Takes out nitrogen from the air.
4. Adjusts the way the air is delivered.
5. Delivers the purified air.

- There are many parts that make up a portable oxygen concentrator. A compressor and sieve bed filter is a couple of the main parts.
- The compressor compresses air that is filtered into the concentrator, then delivers the air in a continuous stream.

- The compressed air moves to the sieve bed filters. The sieve bed filter plays an important role, as it is the device that removes the nitrogen from the air.
- A material called Zeolite, which is a six-sided microscopic cube with holes on each side, is in the sieve bed and this is what removes the nitrogen from the air.
- Two sieve beds are located in the concentrator. After air is first compressed in the concentrator, it is forced into the first sieve bed. Oxygen is sent into the product tank. The first sieve bed then gets filled up with nitrogen.
- Next, the gas flow is switched, and the compressed air is moved to the second sieve bed.
- The first sieve bed's compressor is sent to the outside room, and the air from the product tank goes back into the first sieve bed.
- The drop in pressure from the first sieve bed and the weakening of oxygen make the Zeolite release nitrogen.
- The Oxygen and Nitrogen come back together and are released into the room as regular air. The air is then compressed and sent to the second sieve where Oxygen is moved through it to the Product Tank. The whole cycle starts over again with the first sieve after a few seconds.

Other important parts are the cooling system that keeps the portable oxygen concentrator from overheating, and the nasal cannula that delivers the purified oxygen after the oxygen has been passed through all the sieve bed filters. The cannula helps improve oxygen absorption.

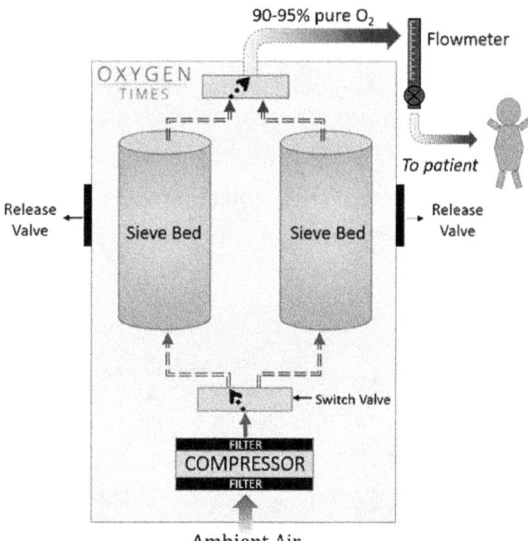

Internal view of the Oxygen Concentrator

- Ambient air (room air) passing through a series of filters is drawn into the machine by a compressor.
- This air is compressed into the 1st molecular sieve bed and all the Nitrogen is adsorbed. The molecular sieve beds are porous & thus have a large surface area due to which they adsorb a large amount of Nitrogen.

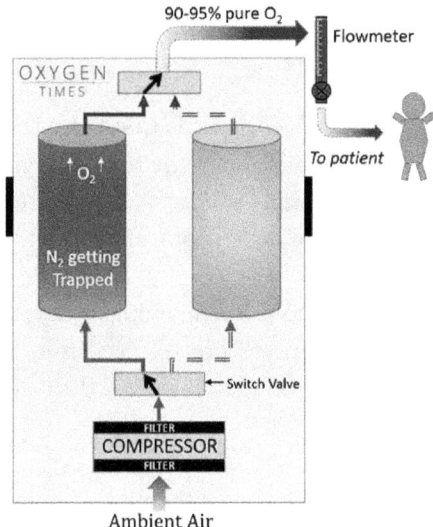

Process

- Now because the air had only Nitrogen and Oxygen as main components; the primary gas that remains is Oxygen.
- This Oxygen has a concentration of up to 95% and is ready to be supplied to the patient via an Oxygen delivery system like Nasal Cannula, Oxygen mask, etc.
- The compressor keeps on compressing air into the 1st molecular sieve bed till it gets saturated (filled) by Nitrogen. The sieve bed usually gets saturated at a pressure of 20 psi.

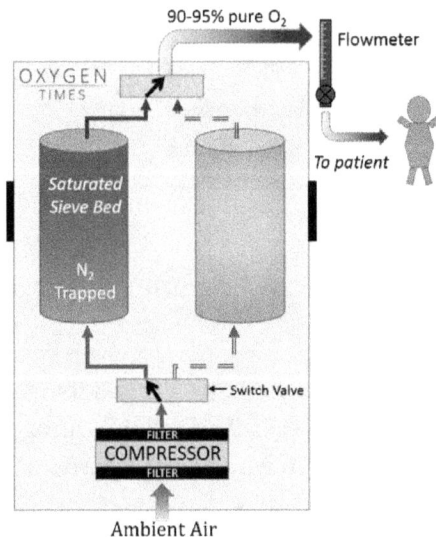

Next Process

- Just before the 1st molecular sieve bed gets saturated, the Switch Valve comes into action, and the output of the air compressor is immediately switched to the 2nd sieve bed i.e. the compressor starts compressing air to the 2nd

molecular sieve.

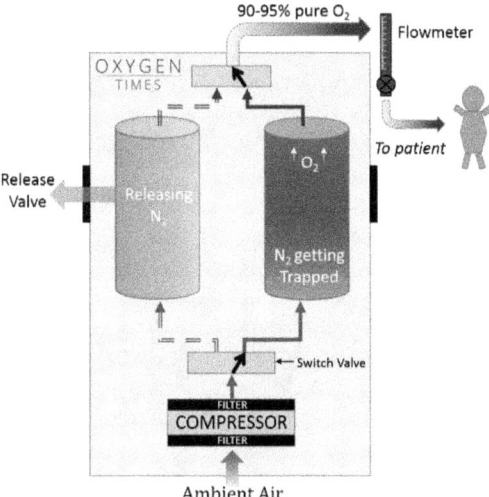

Next Process

- While this sieve bed gets saturated by Nitrogen, the Nitrogen that was trapped in the 1st sieve bed is vented out. The little Nitrogen that is left in the sieve bed after discharging is removed by back-flushing of Oxygen from the other sieve bed.
- The switch valve again switches the output of the air compressor back to the 1st sieve bed as soon as the 2nd sieve bed approaches saturation.

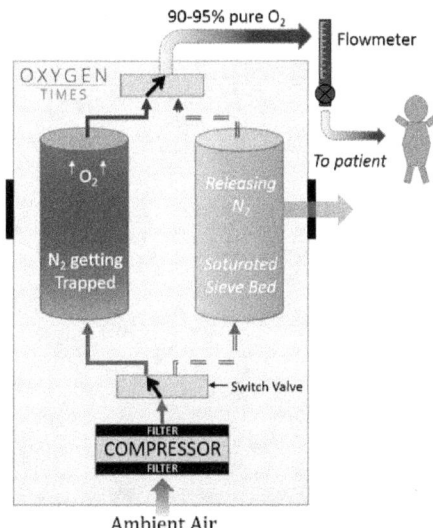

Next Process

- This process keeps on repeating to ensure a continuous flow of Oxygen.

- This process of switching the sieve beds is known as Pressure Swing Adsorption (PSA).
- The output of Oxygen is then controlled using a flowmeter where the flow can be set manually in Litres Per Minute (LPM).
- Oxygen flows out through an outlet where an Oxygen delivery system like a nasal cannula or a mask is usually connected via a humidifier.

CHAPTER FIVE

How to operate the Oxygen Concentrator

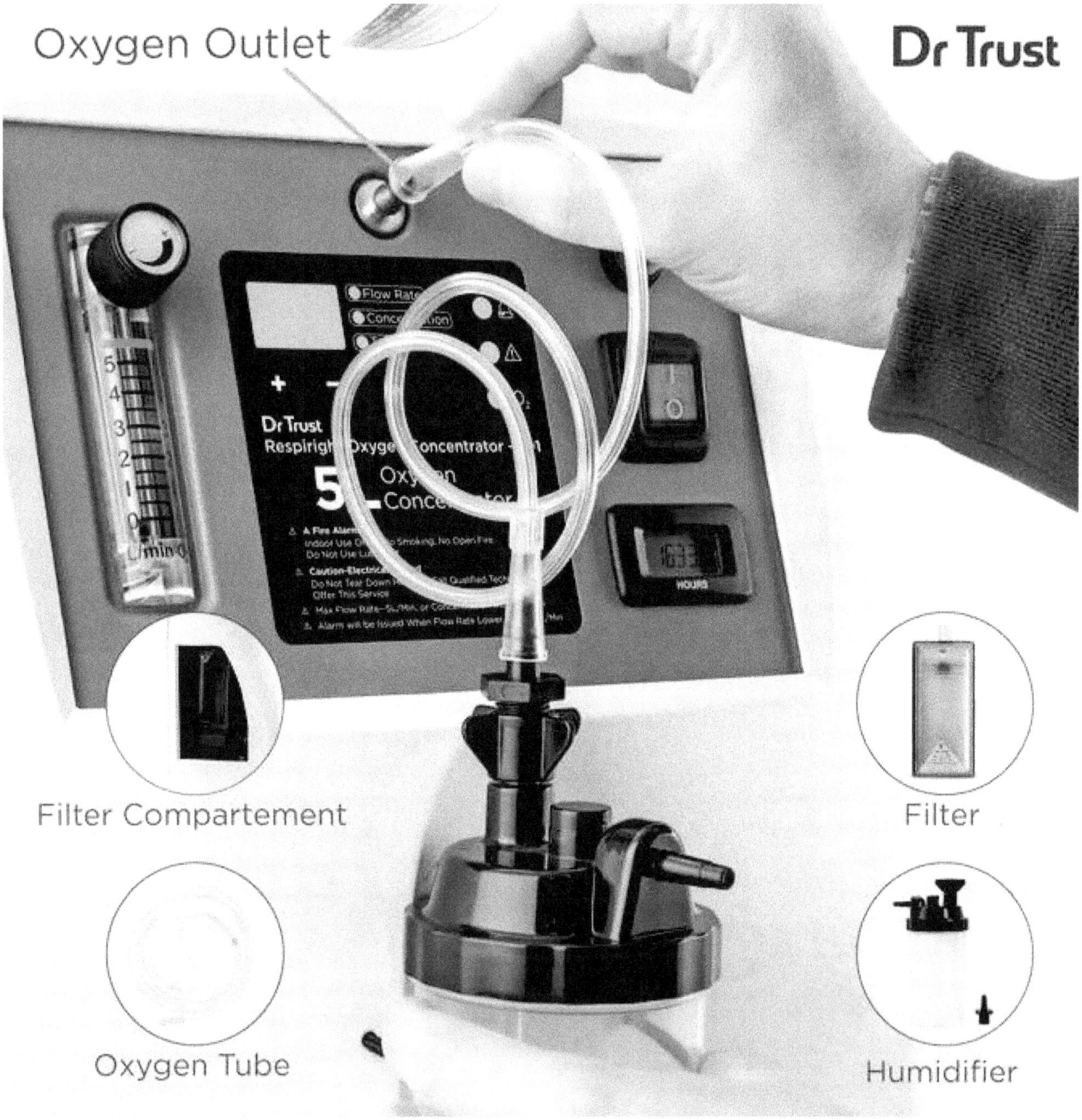

Oxygen Concentrator

OXYGEN CONCENTRATOR

1. Plugin the power supply cable
2. Switch on the concentrator using the ON/OFF button. The green power light will come on.
3. Adjust the flow rate to "4 liters per minute"
4. Adapt the flow-splitter and the calibrated nozzles or use blanking plugs as required.
5. The OSD (oxygen sensor device if present) should show a green light to indicate a normal concentration of oxygen (>90%).
6. Ensure that there are no air leaks
7. Make sure the nose is clear (saline nose drops)
8. Check the Oxygen flow
9. Ensure that the nasal prongs are well fitted to the patient
10. If a pulse oximeter is available, monitor SPO2 along with other vitals

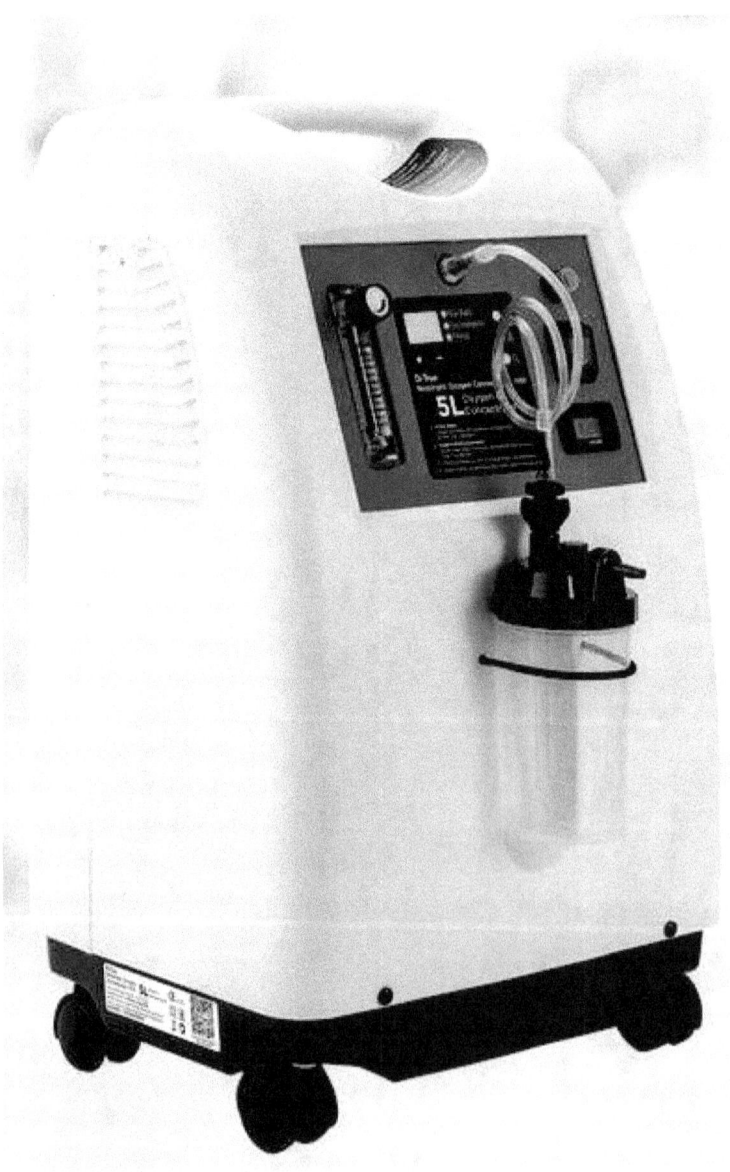

Unscrew The Filter Core Easily For Regular Cleaning of Intake Filter

0.5 to 5 L/min Flow Range at Outlet

Easy to move Around

Oxygen Concentrator

CHAPTER SIX

Advantages of Oxygen Concentrator

- Do you feel like you're always in a mental fog? When you're not getting the oxygen you need, every one of your body's organs is affected; even your brain.
- The first sign that an individual with lung disease isn't getting enough oxygen is confusion. Supplemental oxygen use helps keep your brain and other important organs healthy.
- People who require oxygen therapy are choosing portable oxygen concentrators because they allow them to continue maintaining their standard and quality of life.
- If you're struggling with severe COPD and you have low oxygen levels in your blood, a POC could help you live a healthier, longer life.
- Among the standard treatment approaches for chronic lung diseases like pulmonary fibrosis (PF), chronic obstructive pulmonary disease, and emphysema, supplemental oxygen use at the most advanced stages is often prescribed near-universally.
- While there are other types of medicine used in tandem, like corticosteroids, inhalers, and prescription medicines, supplemental oxygen use has stayed a staple in lung disease treatment for its ability to offer continued respiratory support for individuals struggling with their oxygen intake on a daily level.

www.ingramcontent.com/pod-product-compliance
Lightning Source LLC
LaVergne TN
LVHW081547060526
838200LV00048B/2246